D1473773

You Wouldn't Love Me If You Knew

Abingdon Press

Nashville

You Wouldn't Love Me If You Knew

ISBN 0-687-07325-1

05 06 07 08 09 10 11 12 - 10 9 8 7 6 5 4 3 2

Printed in China

For Bette Nordberg

an encourager who loves unconditionally

Once upon a time a young boy did something very bad. Even though it was a secret and no one else knew, he felt awful.

"I don't like feeling bad," he told his dog.
"From now on, I will do good things."

He picked a bouquet of yellow flowers for his grandmother.

When she saw them, a smile lit her face. "Oh thank you," she said. "I can't get out to pick flowers anymore, and these make the house look beautiful. You are such a good boy."

The boy *said*, "You're welcome," but he *thought*, "I am not good. I am bad. You wouldn't love me if you knew what I did." He felt terrible.

The boy asked his grandfather, "Can I help you Grandpa?"

Grandpa pointed to the tools scattered across the garage floor. "You could pick those up. It's hard for me to bend over."

The boy gathered all the tools and arranged them on the workbench.

His grandfather said, "Thank you. You are a good boy."

The boy *said*, "You're welcome," but he *thought*, "I am not a good boy. I am bad. You wouldn't love me if you knew what I did." He felt worse than ever.

He trudged over to his own house and lay on his tummy,
watching Dad weed the corn.
Each time the pile of weeds grew big, the boy
stuffed them in a plastic lawn bag.

When the job was finished, he dragged the sack of weeds over to the garbage can. Dad beamed with pride.

"Thank you for helping me," he said. "You are a good boy."

The boy *said*, "You're welcome," but he *thought*, "I am not a good boy. I am bad. You wouldn't love me if you knew what I did."

He felt ashamed.

He wandered into the kitchen
to watch his mother knead bread.

"Would you wash the dishes for me?" she asked.
"The soap makes my hands red and itchy."
     The boy jumped up and washed all the dishes.
Then he dried them.
     "Thank you," she said, smiling, "You are such a
good boy."

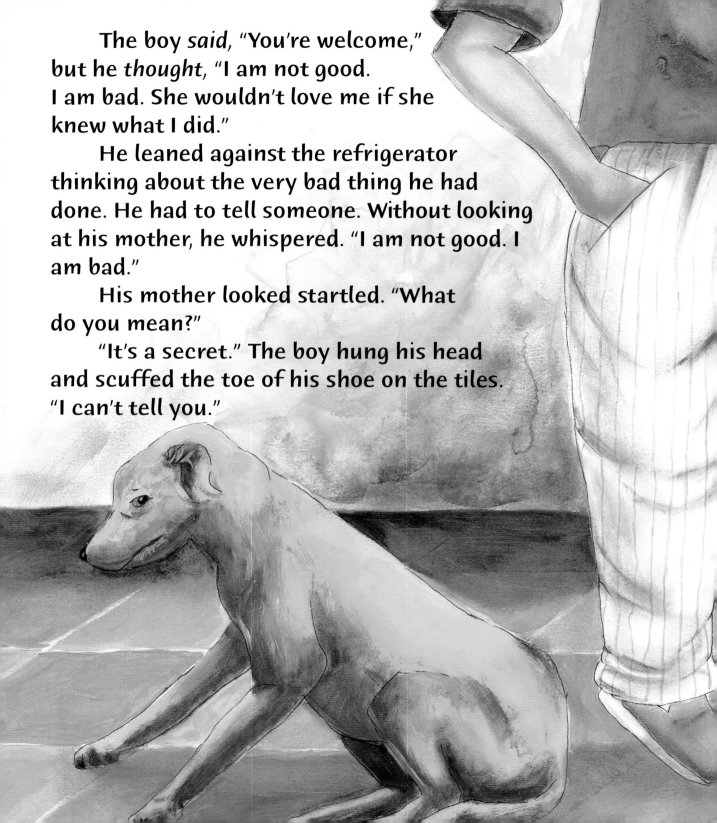

The boy *said*, "You're welcome," but he *thought*, "I am not good. I am bad. She wouldn't love me if she knew what I did."

He leaned against the refrigerator thinking about the very bad thing he had done. He had to tell someone. Without looking at his mother, he whispered. "I am not good. I am bad."

His mother looked startled. "What do you mean?"

"It's a secret." The boy hung his head and scuffed the toe of his shoe on the tiles. "I can't tell you."

"Maybe you should whisper it in my ear." His mother knelt beside him and the boy whispered the very bad thing into her ear. When she heard it, she dropped her head. She looked sad.

Fear pounded in the boy's heart. He thought, "She can't forgive something that bad. Not even Jesus could forgive something that bad. She won't love me anymore."

"Please forgive me," he said.

His mother put her arms around him and pulled him close. "I am sorry you chose to do such a bad thing," she said. "But I am happy you decided to tell me about it and ask for forgiveness. I love you very much.
Of course I forgive you."

"Do you think Jesus could ever forgive something that bad?" asked the boy.

"Jesus will forgive anything—no matter how bad it is. Just ask him."

The boy bowed his head and closed his eyes. "Dear Jesus," he prayed. "I am sorry for what I did. Please forgive me."

He waited a moment, then opened his eyes. He smiled. "I don't feel bad anymore," he said. "I feel good."

He hugged his mother and ran out to play.

For Parents

I hope this book will help children overcome a universal fear. *No one would love m[e]* *if they really knew me.* Children who read this story will identify with the boy. The[n] when questioned about what they think the boy did, they will often name something bad they have done or have been tempted to do. The discussion that ensues will give you the opportunity to assure your child that you will always lov[e] her or him unconditionally.

Talk about it

Ask, "What do you think the young boy in the story did?" You may offer suggestions, but, for the most part, simply listen while your child lists different possibilities. Your child will probably tell you about the very behavior that tempts him or her and may even mention doing something that seems to a child to be unforgivable. Agree that the things your child listed are bad. Then assure your child that you would forgive him or her even if he or she did something that bad.

Take action

Say, "Write down the worst thing you have ever done. No one will see it but you." Talk about the fact that Jesus will forgive any sin—if we ask him. After you pray together for Jesus to forgive the sins your child has written, burn the paper to demonstrate the sin is completely gone. Tell your child that God won't even remember the forgiven sin anymore.

Thank God

Bow your heads and thank God that God always forgives us, no matter what, if w[e] only ask.

In God's love,

Jeannie St. John Taylor